NARRATIVE

OF THE

LIFE

OF

JAMES DOWNING,

(A BLIND MAN,)

LATE

A Private in his Majesty's 20th Regiment of Foot.

WRITTEN BY HIMSELF,

AN EASY VERSE.

Price 2s 6d stitched.

A
NARRATIVE
OF THE
LIFE
OF
JAMES DOWNING.

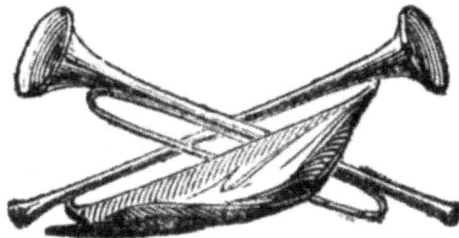

THE AUTHOR'S ACROSTIC.

J esus one day was passing by,
A nd heard two blind men thus to cry,
M ercy of thee we now implore,
E ngage our tender eye-sight to restore.＊
S o great his love, he touch'd their eyes,

D arkness before his presence flies!
O God! thy love was such to me,
W hen I was blind, and could not see;
N ow, Lord, I humbly do confess
I n me thy pow'r has been no less;
N ay, I should still thy name despise,
G reat God! had'st thou not touch'd my eyes.

W hen blind in sin, I stray'd from God,
A nd in the Army went abroad;
S tretching for Egypt there to fight;

B ut here I lost my precious sight,
O ne day when marching on the sand
R egardless, danger was at hand;
N ow suddenly to my surprise,

A blasting wind blew in my eyes.
T hough far from home, and here struck blind,

T he Lord to me was good and kind:
R eturn'd me to my native place,
U nveil'd to me his lovely face:
R ejoice my friends, rejoice with me,
O nce I was blind, but now I see,

I ne'er had sight 'till I was blind,
N or what was good did ever mind.

C ome sinners, in the Gospel way,
O n Jesus call from day to day;
R epeat the blind men's earnest cries,
N ow, Lord in mercy touch my eyes!
W hoever comes shall mercy find,
A ll are invited lame and blind;
L et none thy gracious call despise,
L ord! open thou poor sinners' eyes.

A lmighty and eternal God!
P roclaim thy Sov'reign pow'r abroad,
R estore the Heathen, call the Jew, }
I nfidel, Turk, Barbarian too, }
L ord! none but thou this work can do. }
14th. 1781.

＊Matt. xx. 30—34.

JA:ᴮ DOWNING, AGED 33.

Lost His sight at Alexandria, in Egypt,
in 1801.

A

NARRATIVE

OF THE

LIFE

OF

JAMES DOWNING,

(A BLIND MAN,)

LATE

A Private in his Majesty's 20th Regiment of Foot

CONTAINING

HISTORICAL, NAVAL, MILITARY, MORAL, RELIGIOUS
AND ENTERTAINING REFLECTIONS.

◆

Composed by himself, in easy Verse, and Publishe
at the request of his Friends.

THIRD EDITION.

LONDON:

Printed by J. Haddon, Tabernacle Walk:
And sold by the Author, Chapel Yard, Angel Street, Bedford.

1815.

PREFACE.

THE Author of the following Narrative had lost his sight in the service of his king and country in Egypt; being then a private in his Majesty's 20th Regiment of Foot. But since that period, having, through divine grace, become of a serious turn of mind, has employed himself in recollecting the several incidents of his life and conduct, which he has versified at different times, for his own amusement, and the entertainment of his friends; who have expressed their approbation, and wished him to make it public, as a probable mean of affording him some relief. The Author is not so vain, as to suppose that he has produced a perfect piece of poetry; he therefore begs the candid indulgence of his friends and the public, and hopes they will excuse any errors they may perceive in the composition. He has only to observe in his own behalf, that it is founded on facts and experience, and dictated by the sincerest regard to virtue and truth.

PREFACE TO THE SECOND EDITION.

THE former edition, consisting of 1000 copies, was published in March 1811, the whole of which having been disposed of, and several applications having been since made, the Author is encouraged to reprint the work.

The first edition was published by Subscription, but on this account the Author ventures to publish his feeble performance, relying on the demand of a generous public, who he hopes will give it their sanction and encouragement.

A NARRATIVE, &c.

PART I.

Some account of the Author's early life—his entrance into the Army—Expedition to Holland—reflections on what he there witnessed—his return to England.

READER, I shall attempt to tell,
  My life and actions past,
And speak of his Almighty pow'r,
  Who brought me safe at last.

My birth and parentage relate,
  And how I pass'd my youth,
You soon shall hear, if you'll attend,
  To what I've said in truth.

Whatever error you may see,
  In this my narrative,
I humbly hope your charity,
  And candour will forgive.

In Truro, Cornwall, I was born;
  But soon my mother died;
Thus she by death from me was torn,
  And I had lost my guide.

B

Thus being left in infancy,
    My father labour'd hard;
From any thing which he saw good,
    I never was debarr'd.

He sent me to a neighbouring School,
    Where I was taught to read;
But as in stature I advanc'd,
    In sin I did proceed.

As an apprentice I was bound,
    A shoemaker to be;
To serve my master for five years,
    Before I could be free.

When I had duly serv'd my time,
    And gain'd my liberty,
My inclination soon was bent,
    A soldier then to be.

My friends advised me to stay
    At home, and be content;
But I ne'er heeded their advice,
    So as a soldier went.

To serve in the militia then,
    A substitute I went,
But, ah! how does it grieve me, that
    My time in sin I spent.

In drinking, singing, swearing, too,
    I pass'd my time away:
But now must join the regiment,
    And that without delay.

Then I was march'd to Bodmin Camp,
    To join the Army there,
In rioting and drunkenness,
    My bounty soon grew spare.

Here I could not be satisfied
    My money being spent,
Resolv'd was I some means to try,
    To make myself content.

At length in orders it was read
    That we might volunteer,
And march to Barram Downs with speed,
    To join the sold'ry there.

The expedition there encamp'd,
    For Holland was design'd;
And in the same I volunteer'd,
    To gratify my mind.

Part of my bounty I received,
    And soon was march'd away,
In company with all the rest,
    That volunteer'd that day.

When we arriv'd at Exeter,
    My bounty there was paid;
And in the paths of wickedness,
    Most carelessly I stray'd.

Though only eighteen years of age,
    Just in the bloom of youth,
I practis'd almost every vice,
    And shunn'd the way of truth.

How far from me the thought of death,
  Of judgment or of God ;
Or, on those things I might expect,
  When I was sent abroad.

But here we must no longer stay,
  The General gives command,
That we must march without delay,
  And leave our native land.

In divers sorts of vehicles,
  Then we were quickly sent,
Both night and day, till we arriv'd
  At Deal, a town in Kent.

Now, being at the very place
  Where we must go on board,
I was resolv'd that I would have
  All that I could afford.

But, ah ! my money and my time
  Grew very short indeed,
For we were order'd instantly,
  To go on board with speed.

The transports lay in readiness,
  To bear us all away :
And some of us were sent on board,
  The rest embark'd next day.

But after drinking to excess,
  And now to be debarr'd ;
Was adding grief to my distress,
  I thought it very hard.

But I must leave off all those things,
　To cross the raging seas;
And as a soldier now prepare,
　To meet my enemies.

The vessels soon got under weigh,
　For the Dutch coast did steer,
And after sailing several days,
　We came to anchor there.

Then we were order'd in the boats,
　And taken to the shore;
But many soldiers landed here,
　Who ne'er returned more.

The enemy was driven back,
　Our landing was made good;
Then we refresh'd ourselves awhile,
　And after them pursued.

We then march'd up the sandy beach,
　Drew near to Helder town :
But night advancing on apace,
　Oblig'd us to lay down.

Here we all night lay on the ground,
　Expos'd to wet and cold;
And when the day light did appear,
　New scenes we did behold.

" To arms! To arms!" was now the cry,
　I forward must proceed,
With haste to meet the threat'ning foe,
　Whate'er they had decreed.

Here the contending armies met,
　And many there were slain,
But I was one, among the rest,
　That did in life remain.

Now let us here my friends recount,
　The goodness of the Lord,
Who saved me tho' vile as they,
　From the devouring sword.

He saved me from dangers which
　At once did me surround,
But Oh! with shame I now confess,
　No love to him I found.

No love to God, no love to Christ;
　In what a wretched case
Is miserable fallen man,
　While destitute of grace.

My sole intention in these lines,
　Is to shew forth the praise
And loving kindness of that God,
　Who lengthen'd out my days.

'Twas he who gave me breath at first,
　And has prolong'd my days,
That I might in some future time,
　Shew forth his heav'nly praise.

That I might shew his praises forth,
　While life and being last,
Be kept by his almighty power,
　And brought to heav'n at last.

But let us turn awhile and view
  The state that I was in,
Far distant from my native home,
  And blindly bold in sin.

Here we were march'd from town to town,
  Against our enemies,
Scarce any rest by day or night,
  Or slumber for my eyes.

Some times we laid on the cold ground,
  Some times in barns on hay,
Some nights, we laid on the sand hills,
  Until the break of day.

And when the morning light appear'd,
  New scenes did it attend,
And I in reason could not think,
  That I the day should end.

Here I, this morning may converse;
  With one who is my friend,
But ah! before the ev'ning comes,
  His days are at an end.

Alas, my friend is nothing more
  Than a dead lump of clay,
And his remains in dust must lie,
  Until the judgment day.

How frail is man, how soon cut off,
  And summon'd to appear
Before the Judge of quick and dead,
  To meet his sentence there.

But oh! my friends with shame I speak,
  So ignorant was I,
I thought, if I dy'd in the field,
  My soul to heav'n would fly.

Yet when the balls began to fly,
  It shook my very frame,
My conduct star'd me in the face,
  I felt remorse and shame.

Those thoughts did not continue long,
  They'd quickly disappear,
And when I was in danger most,
  Then I was void of fear.

One day as I was order'd out
  To meet my enemies,
Advancing on by the sea side,
  An object met my eyes:

Here I beheld an Officer,
  Just gasping out his breath,
A ball had pierced him through the breast,
  And brought him down to death.

Not far from him a private lay;
  Rank'd with the silent dead,
Stretch'd on the ground, upon his face:
  A spear ran through his head.

Death's arrows all at random flew,
  And made no diff'rence here,
For Officers and private men,
  Alike the same did share.

We read in scripture of King Saul,
　That he hath thousands slain,
And David tens of thousands too,
　But thousands yet remain.

Alas! what mischief sin hath done,
　What millions hath it kill'd;
Sin, Sin hath been the only cause,
　Of all the blood that's spill'd.

Thus having finish'd these remarks,
　I on my way proceed;
For I, from Holland must return
　To England, with all speed.

Then we proceeded on our march,
　Along by the sea side,
There being now no other way,
　To march to shun the tide.

The road was very rough indeed,
　We marched near the sea,
Because upon the other side,
　Large rocks, and sand hills lay.

Night coming on, it grew quite dark;
　This much distress'd us then,
Because the road was dang'rous now,
　To march so many men.

The raging sea made awful noise,
　No rest that night I found,
A wave assail'd me on the beach,
　And I was nearly drown'd.

Here I an Ebenezer raise,
　To God who was my friend,
Who in the time of deep distress,
　Did great assistance lend.

But oh! the hardness of my heart,
　That I did not return
My thanks to God, who was my friend,
　Nor for my sins did mourn.

Sure if the Lord had cut me off,
　And from his presence thrust
Me down to hell, there to remain;
　His judgments would be just.

For here his mercy and his love,
　His judgments, follow'd me;
But in these great deliv'rances,
　His hand I could not see.

Next morning we arrived at
　Ekmountupzee, a town,
Where we in barns, and houses went,
　Awhile to lay us down.

Being much fatigu'd I thought to rest,
　But I was now debarr'd,
A Corporal call'd, and bid me rise;
　For I must go on guard.

Eleven of our company,
　Were wounded in the fight,
And by assistance they were brought
　Back to the town that night.

Our Colonel had receiv'd a wound
  Our Adjutant likewise,
Our Major was shot from his horse;
  In death he clos'd his eyes.

But through the mercy of the Lord,
  I did in life remain,
And was preserv'd by him, and brought
  Safe back on board again.

But now to trace his goodness more
  I homeward must proceed,
We re-embark'd, and then set sail
  For England with all speed.

I thought all dangers now were past,
  To meet with them no more,
I thought, what pleasures I should have
  When I got safe on shore.

But when we think ourselves secure,
  The danger is most near,
For this was now the case with me,
  As quickly you shall hear.

The wind blew strong, the sea was rough,
  Yet we no danger spy'd,
'Till we ran foul another ship,
  And fasten'd to her side.

She was superior in size,
  The sea was very high,
Which put us in a dreadful fright,
  For death seem'd very nigh.

In this distress upon the waves,
   We up and down were toss'd,
Expecting every wave that roll'd,
   That we should all be lost.

Our seamen labour'd very hard,
   Not heeding care or pain;
And every effort now was us'd
   To get us clear again.

At length our Captain gave the word
   To cut the ropes away;
This being done, we soon got clear,
   And bore away to sea.

Once more from danger I was freed
   By His all gracious hand,
Who did appear in my behalf,
   By sea as well as land.

But oh! I did not see that hand,
   Which was stretch'd forth to save,
Which rescu'd me the second time,
   From the devouring wave.

No sooner was the danger o'er,
   Then all things seem'd to smile,
And promis'd that I soon should be
   Quite free from care and toil.

We steer'd our coasts for Yarmouth roads;
   The wind blew strong and fair,
And in the space of a few days,
   We safe arrived there.

When we cast anchor in the roads,
　I long'd to be on shore,
That I might to my vice return,
　Nor think of dangers more.

Our boats were quickly hoisted out,
　And we were sent on shore,
I landed safe at Yarmouth, where
　I never was before.

My friends, this is a brief account,
　Of my first voyage abroad,
In which you plainly may perceive
　The goodness of the Lord.

His goodness follow'd me abroad,
　And safely brought me home :
But you will see his goodness more,
　In what is yet to come.

END OF PART ONE.

PART II.

Some account of the removal of the Regiment from Yarmouth in Norfolk, to Ashford in Kent, and the circumstances which occurred by the way—Voyage to Ireland—dangerous situation in a storm—safe arrival at the Cove of Cork—manner of living during their continuance in that City.

AT Yarmouth we in quarters went,
　As you shall understand,
But here my time was badly spent,
　I sinn'd with a high hand.

I drank down sin fast as the ox
　Doth water, when athirst;
In almost every common sin,
　I then strove to be first.

For drunkenness, and swearing too
　Sure there could never be,
After so many mercies past,
　A sinner vile as me.

I soon forgot the gracious hand,
　And long forbearance too,
Of Him who always was my friend,
　And safely brought me through.

'Tis here his Justice would have shone,
  If he had cut me down;
And doom'd me to that place of woe,
  To dwell beneath his frown.

But oh! his love to me was great,
  My worthless life to spare,
When Justice would have cut me down,
  His mercy cried, " forbear."

But turn again, behold a wretch
  Who did not stand in awe,
But still went on defying God,
  And trampling on his law.

We soon for Norwich city march'd,
  My heart in sin was bent,
And there we did receive the rout,
  For Ashford town in Kent.

Three days we in this place remain'd,
  Where I receiv'd my pay,
Which I in Holland had procur'd,
  By toiling night and day.

But though I won it by fatigue,
  Upon the land and sea,
I soon expended what I had,
  Nor car'd for poverty.

Proceeding onward in our march
  With speed from town to town,
An awful circumstance occur'd,
  Which I shall here note down—

As an example unto all
  Who in their sins proceed,
And carried captive by the same,
  Do end their days with speed.

This was the case with a young man,
  Then in our regiment,
Whose heart like mine, on drunkenness
  Continually was bent.

As he was on our baggage guard,
  With liquor in his care,
Of it he drank to such excess,
  That he expired there.

He fell a victim to that sin,
  Which numbers more hath slain;
And was it not amazing love,
  That I did still remain?

While this young man was thus cut off,
  And summon'd to appear
Before the Judge of all the earth,
  To meet his sentence there:

'Twas boundless mercy that preserv'd,
  And kept me at that time,
Or I had been like that young man,
  Cut off when in my prime.

But I will on my march proceed,
  That you the more may see
How good and gracious was the Lord
  To such a wretch as me.

We soon at Ashford town ariv'd,
　And went in Barracks there;
It being now December month,
　The weather was severe.

What pay I had was almost spent,
　But Christmas drawing nigh,
To get some more against that time,
　I every means did try.

And thus when Christmas day was come,
　It being frost and snow,
I thought upon my friends at home,
　Which made me bolder grow.

I went and ask'd my Officer
　Some liberty and pay,
That I might from all duty free,
　Enjoy the Christmas day.

At my request he gave me leave,
　And order'd me some pay,
Then to the ale house I did go,
　To spend the Christmas day.

Should any ask why all this mirth,
　To them it would be said,
Our Saviour Christ was born to day,
　And in a manger laid.

A sad and dreadful way indeed,
　To celebrate the birth,
Of Christ the only Son of God,
　Who came from heav'n to earth.

I little thought it at that time,
　　When full of sin and pride,
That by the Saviour's life and death,
　　I must be justified.

That he on him my nature took,
　　To suffer, bleed, and die,
Upon the cross on Calv'ry's top,
　　For such a wretch as I.

Not any saving views of Christ,
　　Had ever reach'd my heart,
For I did love my sins so well,
　　From them I could not qart.

But here I would one thing remark,
　　Which happen'd in this place,
To shew the wretched state of man,
　　While destitute of grace.

One of the soldiers in this place,
　　A married man he was,
He, and his wife, one day fell out,
　　And soon they came to blows.

This man was so implacable,
　　So passionate and hot,
He struck his wife a dreadful blow,
　　Which kill'd her on the spot.

He was immediately confin'd,
　　To lodgings cold and hard,
Which much affected each of us
　　Who were that night on guard.

That night the snow was very deep,
  His groans by us were heard,
Which made us all resolve to ask
  The captain of the guard—

To let him come in the guard-room,
  And warm him by the fire;
He paid respect to our request,
  And granted our desire.

To see the anguish of his mind
  Was an affecting sight,
It was not fire nor company,
  Could yield the least delight!

He walked to and fro the room,
  His trouble now was great,
He for his folly did repent,
  But it was now—too late.

" Alas! he cried, my wife is dead,
  " And I must shortly die ;
" Was ever man in such a case,
  " Why was I born, Oh! why?"

Early next morn the chaise was brought
  Which took him to the goal;
I leave him there, and pray that God
  May bless his precious soul.

Let us reflect on this poor man,
  Whenever passion rise,
And pray for grace to check the same,
  Nor rest till passion dies.

Our reason falls an easy prey,
    When passion is let loose ;
Our kindred, yea, our dearest friends,
    Come under our abuse.

'Twas passion influenc'd wicked Cain,
    To slay his pious brother ;
Oh ! may this sin in us be slain,
    Lest we slay one another.

O Lord, pour down thy heav'nly grace,
    Check passion in its bud ;
And wash our guilty stains away,
    In thy atoning blood.

In Ashford I was not content
    To be so much confin'd ;
I was from liberty debarr'd,
    This did not please my mind.

I wish'd myself once more away,
    To meet the foe again,
Rather than be confin'd at home,
    Or in this place remain.

It vas not long before we had
    The rout to march away ;
And this was welcome news indeed,
    Yea, a rejoicing day.

One horning, as we march'd to field,
    With all the music band ;
A horse-man rode up with the rout,
    " For Cork in Ireland."

Our Major when he heard the same,
  Dismiss'd us all straightway,
To get our things in readiness,
  To march th' ensuing day.

We got all things in readiness
  Next morn by break of day;
Paraded in the barrack-yard,
  Prepar'd to march away.

I march'd away from Ashford, with
  A perfect willing mind;
And thence was sent on board at Deal,
  To sail the first fair wind.

That day to Canterbury march'd,
  The next we reached Deal,
And then embark'd on board the ships,
  For Ireland to sail.

And as we pass'd by the Land's end,
  Strong blew the wind and fair;
There I the hills of Cornwall saw,
  And wish'd that I was there.

But I must leave my native land,
  And hasten now to tell,
The dangers of this voyage at sea,
  And what to us befell.

To think of home was all in vain.
  While duty calls away;
And I was once more here expos'd,
  To dangers on the sea.

Fair was the wind, the weather fair,
  When we put out to sea;
And on the third day we espy'd,
  The rocks on Bantry bay.

As night was coming on apace,
  Our Captain bore away,
In hopes that we should reach the Cove,
  On the ensuing day.

But all our hopes were quickly lost,
  For it must be remark'd,
That we were one and twenty days,
  Before we disembark'd.

The wind sprang up from off the shore,
  The sea ran very high;
Which drove us off so far to sea,
  That we no land could spy.

Our vessel sail'd so very fast,
  Leaving the rest behind;
Near thirteen knots an hour we went,
  Before the driving wind.

So roughly was she tossed about,
  And beaten by the waves,
That now to keep the water out
  We ply'd like Galley slaves.

Alternately at the chain pumps,
  Each was oblig'd to be,
Not knowing when the night came on,
  That we the day should see.

Not any reck'ning could we keep,
  Which did our fear increase;
Not knowing where the ship might drive,
  Or when the storm would cease.

Sometimes we roll'd upon the waves
  Though they ran mountains high;
Sometimes so low between the same,
  That ruin seemed nigh.

For fourteen days we thus were lost,
  Fatigued day and night:
At length one morning we perceiv'd
  A sail appear in sight.

Our hearts within us did rejoice,
  When we the barn did see,
Though we were greatly unprepar'd,
  To meet an enemy.

The drums to quarters now did beat,
  To arms we must repair;
Our seamen did exert themselves,
  To get the decks quiet clear.

A shot we fired from our ship,
  She to the same did bend,
But as it nearer did approach,
  We found she was a friend.

She was a brig from Liverpool,
  To America was bound,
This caus'd us greatly to rejoice,
  That we such friends had found.

The raging waves grew still more calm,
  The storm did much abate,
And this reviv'd our drooping hearts,
  From our impending fate.

The captain told us where we were,
  This much reviv'd my heart,
When we each other wish'd good speed,
  And then from them did part.

Now we for Cork did once more sail,
  The wind not very fair,
Yet in the space of four whole days
  We safe arrived there.

The boats now got in readiness,
  We gladly went on board;
And when we got all safe on shore,
  Much joy it did afford.

Then from the dangers of the sea,
  I once more here was freed,
By him who was a present help,
  In every time of need.

Now there was reason to expect,
  I should begin to praise
The God of all my mercies past,
  Who lengthen'd out my days.

But now my treach'rous wicked heart
  Was so much bent on sin,
That I had scarce set foot on shore,
  Before I did begin.

To follow my whole course of life,
    And to forget the hand
Which sav'd me from the threat'ning waves,
    And brought me safe to land.

When we arrived at the Cove,
    We did expect to find
The other ship, which in the storm
    We left so far behind.

We found that she was not arriv'd,
    Which caused us to fear,
That she by reason of the storm,
    The weather could not bear.

Part of our regiment was on board,
    Which now did grieve us sore,
To think we in the storm did part,
    Perhaps to meet no more!

We straightway marched into Cork,
    Where we were quarter'd round,
And greatly did I then rejoice,
    I such refreshment found.

My quarters here were very good,
    This much reliev'd my mind,
They brought to us both drink and food
    And acted very kind.

Then, as I had refresh'd myself,
    My business next must be,
A walk to take into the streets,
    For curiosity.

D

My next concern was to procure,
　　If possible, some pay,
That I might at the alehouse spend
　　The remnant of the day.

I at the alebench spent the day,
　　Then to my quarters went :
But I must now return again
　　Unto the regiment.

Next morn we on parade appear'd
　　And then were much reviv'd,
For now the news was brought to us,
　　The ship was safe arriv'd!

As we our comrades marched in,
　　What pleasure ' was to see,
The friends we thought for ever lost,
　　Once more from danger free.

When we were thus together met,
　　We told of dangers past ;
And mutually rejoic'd to see
　　Each other safe at last.

What pleasure was it then to us,
　　We now could have some sleep,
After the restless nights we spent,
　　Upon the wat'ry deep.

We soon from quarters were remov'
　　Into the barracks there ;
And order'd when on the parade,
　　Like Soldiers to appear.

And when the Sabbath day was come,
　For church we did perpare ;
As if to battle we were call'd,
　Just so we marched there.

When we arriv'd at the church door,
　Our Colonel then commands
That all our muskets we should keep
　Securely in our hands.

For fear the rebels should attempt
　To take our lives away,
We might be found in readiness
　To meet them night or day.

Though the rebellion then had ceas'd,
　And things more quiet grew
There was a number in the this place
　That would us mischief do.

The envy of their treach'rous hearts,
　To us was very bad;
For they would slay us privately
　If they occasion had.

Here we beheld the sad effects
　Of what before was done,
Which made us be upon our guard,
　Their company to shun.

Here in the streets the heads hung up
　Of those who had been slain,
As great examples for the rest,
　Who did in life remain.

It being in the winter time,
  The weather was severe ;
But what increas'd our misery,
  Provisions grew so dear.

From February until June,
  We in this place did stay,-
When things grew so immensely dear,
  I wish'd myself away.

For now my mind on drunkenness,
  So very much was set,
That I could not tell what to do,
  More money how to get.

The times were grown so very hard,
  That I could have no pay,
So that I was oblig'd to be
  Sober, both night and day.

Thus I grew weary of this place,
  And wished every day,
That orders might be quickly brought,
  For us to march away.

At length to us the route was brought,
  The same did joy afford;
Then soon all things we did prepare,
  Once more to go on board.

Next morn we on parade appear'd,
  And march'd down to the quay,
Where all the boats were then prepar'd,
  To carry us away.

With joy we went on board the boats,
  And left this place behind,
Then we embark'd on board the ships,
  To sail the first fair wind.

Where we were bound we could not tell,
  But this was all our cry,
We'd rather be on board a ship,
  Than stay behind to die.

END OF THE SECOND PART.

PART III.

Account of the voyage from Ireland to the Mediterranean—Expedition to Spain—engagement of Ferrol—blockade of Cadiz—departure from Spain—arrival at the Island of Minorca, some account of the superstitious ceremonies of its inhabitants.

IN a short time the wind blew fair,
  Our anchor we did weigh,
Then soon we sail'd out of the Cove,
  And bore away to sea.

There was another ship with us,
  That had our men on board,
Each of them carried thirty guns,
  Which might relief afford.

If we by chance our foes should meet,
  When sailing on the waves,
We were resolv'd to fight our way,
  Rather than be their slaves.

We soon once more lost sight of land
  To cross the raging main,
But we had sev'ral men on board,
  That ne'er saw land again.

Some of our men were taken ill,
   No doctor's skill could save;
Some of them died, and soon were launch'd
   Into a watery grave.

Though men were snatch'd off every side,
   It did not me affect,
To all the warnings of the Lord,
   I then had no respect.

The burial of the dead at sea,
   Most solemn did appear,
Yet so impenitent was I,
   As not to shed a tear.

Soldiers and sailors both stood by,
   With hat and cap in hand,
The funeral service was perform'd,
   Much as it is on land.

The corpse was on a grating laid—
   What could more striking be?
A sand bag fasten'd to its feet,
   To sink it in the sea.

" Commit this body to the deep,"
   The chaplain gave the word,
The same was instantly obey'd
   And then launch'd over board.

And here I'm at a loss to tell,
   The state that I was in,
For I was never satisfied,
   But when engag'd in sin.

If soldiers were but men of grace,
 And inward piety;
What contemplation would they have,
 On those things which they see.

For they can see the works of God
 Shine forth in brighter rays,
Than those that always stay at home,
 And never cross the seas.

For when I sometimes do reflect
 On things which I have seen,
I often think within myself,
 Where could my thoughts have been,

That I had not improv'd those things
 Presented to my view,
And that I never had perceiv'd,
 The hand that brought me through.

Since Adam in the garden fell,
 And ate forbidden fruit,
Our ignorance and pride have sunk,
 The man below the brute.

But let us once more trace the hand
 Of God, who was my guide
In every danger that appear'd,
 And did for me provide.

Now as we steer'd our course along,
 No enemy was nigh;
The man spake to us from the top,
 And said he land could spy.

Lo! this was Gibraltar's Rock,
  Which here appear'd in sight,
And then we made what sail we could,
  To reach before 'twas night.

Soon we arrived at this place,
  And anchor'd for the night,
But when the day-light did appear,
  O what a wond'rous sight!

To see this rock so very high,
  What batteries there were form'd
I thought it never could be took,
  However it was storm'd.

To see these guns all rear'd along,
  On man's destruction bent,
Sure if we think of sin aright,
  Here's reason to lament.

To see what sin for man hath done,
  It brings on death and pain,
For by those instruments of war,
  How many have been slain.

This rock, tho' firm, by man was took,
  After much blood was spilt;
But foes can ne'er destroy that rock,
  On which the Church is built.

Though all the host of hell combine,
  This rock doth firm abide;
And Jesus, like a conqueror sits
  Down at his Father's side.

We only tarried here one night,
  And part of the next day,
When orders to our men were brought,
  That we must put to sea.

Now for the coast of Barbary,
  We straight away did steer,
Intending when we reach'd that place,
  To take in water there.

Our vessels having reach'd the Bay,
  We came to anchor there,
And then to take in water, then
  Did instantly prepare.

Our men soon went into the boats,
  And row'd towards the beach,
But here the Moors came flocking down,
  Before these boats could reach.

And they had lances in their hands,
  Their persons to defend;
These weapons they could skilfully
  Cast to effect their end.

Now we made signals unto them,
  That we were real friends;
And if they would us water give,
  We would make them amends.

Soon they our meaning understood,
  And then their signals made,
That we might come and water have,
  And they would with us trade.

Here knives, and buttons, we exchang'd
  And gave to them for fruit,
And thus we traded several days,
  Without the least dispute.

We kept a guard of men on shore,
  To see when both did deal;
That they, nor us, should not intrude,
  Nor from each other steal.

For they were of a savage kind,
  And always bore their lance,
And if you went to deal with one,
  A number would advance.

Now having got our water in,
  Our anchor we did weigh,
And left the Barbary coast behind,
  And bore away to sea.

For th' Isle of Howet we set sail,
  And thither we did steer,
n order there to join the troops,
  Which then were lying there.

When at this place we did arrive,
  We soon were put on shore,
And pitch'd our tents, and form'd a Cam
  With several regiments more.

This was a very pleasant spot,
  Surrounded with the sea,
Yet there were many of our men,
  Fell sick from day to day.

We tarried here about three days,
  Then went on board again;
And all the sick which were on shore,
  We left there to remain.

I had the ague at that time,
  And when on board I came;
Some of my comrades and myself,
  The Doctor call'd by name.

And when he had examin'd us,
  His kind directions were,
That I with several other men,
  Must to the Island steer—

And there to tarry with the sick;
  But if we should revive,
We then were to take care of those
  Who should remain alive.

Some of our men a fever had,
  Which did affect their brain,
And some there were that sicken'd then,
  That ne'er got well again.

Besides the yellow fever, then
  Did in our camp appear,
But out of several regiments,
  But two fell victims there.

Now here the Lord was good to me,
  That I did here remain,
For in a very little time,
  I did get well again.

After remaining several weeks,
　　Our sick men grew more strong,
So then we join'd the twenty third,
　　And did not tarry long.

For soon the fleet to us arriv'd,
　　Which vessels took us all,
To join the expedition then,
　　And go against Ferrol.

Now having all got safe on board,
　　We sailed with the fleet;
And steer'd our course towards Ferrol,
　　Our enemies to meet.

And after we had sail'd awhile,
　　The Spanish coasts we spy'd;
When we to meet our enemies,
　　Did all things soon provide.

This harbour like a bason was,
　　Fenc'd partly round by land;
Our foes could not see our approach,
　　'Till we were near at hand.

Now when we safe had made the point,
　　At once we rushed in,
When they to fire upon our ships,
　　Did instantly begin.

They had an eight-gun battery form'd
　　Upon a lofty beach;
But when they first commenc'd their fire,
　　They found us out of reach.

E

Here we had got some ships of war,
  Which manfully did fight;
The Viper cutter, she was here,
  And London, ninety-eight.

Now while we got into the boats,
  And row'd towards the shore,
These ships so kept their firing up,
  Our foes could do no more.

They spik'd their guns and ran away,
  So left us there to land,
But here the rocks were all so rough,
  That we could hardly stand.

Then we were forc'd to climb the rocks,
  Upon our hands and knees,
Not knowing but we should be beat
  Back by our enemies.

But when that we had reach'd the top,
  Our foes had taken flight,
So we were order'd there to lie
  Upon our arms that night.

We'd cannons landed from our ships,
  To take along with us,
But now the roads were here so rough,
  Our cannons were no use.

Then back on board the guns were sent,
  As now no use to us,
Because to get them up the rocks,
  We here no means could use.

Here many Soldiers and marines,
    Were sent on shore that night,
In order then to march with us,
    To help us in the fight.

Now there were two large batteries,
    At this end of the town:
So that our ships would not attempt
    To go to beat it down.

For here the river was so straight,
    And batteries each side lay,
That if our ships had made attempt,
    They would be beat away.

So they were forced to remain,
    At th' place where we did land,
To see when we our foes did meet,
    If we could them withstand.

Or, if we should be forc'd to run,
    And backwards to recede,
They might endeavour here to take
    Us all on board with speed.

We lay impatient all that night,
    Until the rising morn,
Then we were order'd to advance,
    Through fields of standing corn.

Because the way was much too strait,
    And very rough indeed;
Besides the hills were all so steep,
    That we could scarce proceed.

E 2

From ev'ry house that we pass'd by,
　The men had took their flight,
And we suppose they went to join
　Their army in the night.

Their wives and children here were left,
　In this distress behind,
Sure here is cause for sympathy,
　To ev'ry thoughtful mind.

To see the sad effects of war,
　Men from their fam'lies torn,
And leave their wives and children dear,
　In deep distress to mourn.

O! cruel war, when wilt thou cease;
　When shall thy sword return,
And nations bow themselves in dust,
　Their num'rous sins to mourn?

When shall the happy tidings come,
　That peace is safe arriv'd;
Then nations shall join hand in hand,
　And commerce be reviv'd.

But oh! to war I must return,
　Tho' peace is most desir'd,
For we had not advanced far,
　Before our enemies fir'd.

They form'd themselves behind a hill,
　And thus advantage took,
But when we after them pursu'd,
　They soon this place forsook.

They fired sev'ral shots at us,
  But would not meet us then,
And with those shots the mischief was,
  They wounded several men.

Now as we fired, they drew back,
  And soon we ran them down;
Here some of them we pris'ners took,
  And brought them to the town.

Now soon the firing it was ceas'd,
  And here we did sit down
For to refresh ourselves, and then
  To go against the town.

Here was much honey in this place,
  Of which our men did eat,
And while we thus refresh'd ourselves,
  We'd orders to retreat.

Now soon we left this place behind,
  And march'd towards the beach,
But here the night came on space,
  Ere we that place could reach.

We march'd the pris'ners back with us,
  So left them to remain
Until we all got safe on board,
  Then let them go again.

Here we in great confusion were
  Because we had our fears,
Whether our foes might not return,
  And take us unawares.

The boats were dash'd so with the waves,
 We fear'd we should be drown'd,
So that we all did much rejoice,
 When we our ships had found.

Here I once more would call to mind,
 The goodness of the Lord,
Who in this place preserved me,
 And brought me safe on board.

Now having all things quite secure,
 For Cadiz we did steer;
And we from Gibraltar had
 Some gun boats join us there.

Now when this city we perceiv'd,
 'Twas pleasant to behold,
But then to see how it was fenc'd,
 It made our blood run cold.

Now here our ships drew up in line,
 And rear'd themselves along,
To guard our boats safe to the shore,
 Because the place was strong.

Three days' provision was prepar'd,
 The boats brought along side,
And we to go on shore that night,
 Did all things here provide.

A flag of truce came off that night,
 And things were so agreed,
That we should take our boats on board,
 And go to sea with speed.

Next morning we the same obey'd,
   Our anchors we did weigh,
And took in all our boats on board,
   And bore away to sea.

We sail'd and left the place behind,
   For Vigo we did steer,
And soon we enter'd Vigo Bay,
   And came to anchor there.

As I was here one night to watch,
   The moon shone very clear,
A serjeant came upon the deck,
   To breathe a purer air.

Who could have thought his time so short,
   He scarce refreshment found,
Before he fell into the sea,
   And instantly was drown'd!

Now here we did exert ourselves,
   If we this man could save;
But our attempts were all in vain,
   The sea became his grave.

How fleeting is the life of man,
   How very soon he's hurl'd,
Though in the midst of health and strength,
   Into another world !

There to appear before that God
   Who first gave man his birth,
To give a just account of all
   The deeds he did on earth.

What instances do soldiers see,
   Of sudden deaths around,
Some on the land are snatch'd away,
   Some in the seas are drown'd.

Oh ! if like David they would cry,
   " Lord, number out my days,"
That we may set out hearts on thee,
   And so shew forth thy praise.

Teach us how long we have to live,
   Forgive our sins now past,
And let us live each day to thee.
   As if it were our last.

If this was but a soldier's pray'r,
   Put up from day to day,
They would enjoy a heav'n below,
   By land as well as sea.

For then if sudden death should come,
   Then glory they would find,
And leave the noisy scenes of war,
   And a vain world behind.

The Captain of Salvation would
   Receive them to the skies,
And when they reach'd that blissful place,
   They would receive the prize.

They shall a crown of glory have,
   There plac'd upon their head,
And praise the goodness, love, and pow'r
   Of him who wept and bled.

They shall another dress put on,
    Which cost a greater price,
Than that they wore while here on earth,
    The righteousness of Christ.

But things with us were quite reverse,
    And shameful thus to tell,
I still went headlong down the road
    That leads to death and hell.

Though many awful instances
    Had been before my eyes ;
Though God hath call'd to me by death,
    His calls I did despise.

Though I to danger was expos'd
    Upon the land and seas,
My language was, I do not want
    The knowledge of thy ways.

I acted here like one who thought
    To live on earth always,
As if there were no judgement day,
    Nor yet an end of days.

But let me here once more revere
    The Lord's all-gracious hand,
Who caus'd the billows then to rise,
    And swell at his command.

While we remain'd at Vigo Bay,
    The wind came on one night ;
And here the storm did so increase,
    It did us sore affright.

The sailors here had got no time,
　　Our anchors then to weigh,
Before our cable went in two,
　　And we drove off to sea.

The ships were from their mooring driven,
　　And mournful thus to hear,
The bells on board the ships did ring
　　In order to keep clear.

This was a dreadful night indeed,
　　We up and down were toss'd,
Not knowing every wave that roll'd,
　　But we should all be lost.

Now when day light once appear'd,
　　This did us much relieve,
But when we look'd towards the shore,
　　Then we began to grieve.

One of our frigates, she was blown
　　Upon the Spanish shore,
And here we insantly perceiv'd,
　　We should have her no more.

The Spaniards came flocking down,
　　This vessel to receive ;
Which caus'd us to exert ourselves,
　　The ships' crew to relieve.

Then we towards her did advance.
　　And fired on the shore,
Which made the Spaniards run away,
　　And so return'd no more.

Our men got quickly in the boats,
　And they were toss'd about,
But after tolling for some time,
　They got the men safe out.

So here the Spaniards were deceiv'd,
　And could not have the prize,
For soon they might look down and see
　Her burn before their eyes !

Before the captain left the ship
　He set her all on fire ;
And soon she blew up in the sea,
　For this was our desire.

For having got the men on board,
　We then were satisfied,
Because her loss was not so great
　As if one man had died.

The sov'reign ruler of the world,
　Once more his pow'r display'd,]
In saving us from deep distress,
　When were much afraid.

All things are under his controul,
　In heaven, earth, and seas,
He bids the storm become a calm,
　Or rise whene'er he please.

The guilty man with horror shrinks,
　Fears his avenging rod,
Conscious that he is not prepar'd
　To meet a righteous God.

Who will take vengeance on the man,
  That doth not him obey;
However he may be employ'd
  Upon the land or sea.

Now here our ships were put about,
  We sailed back again,
And we were much surpris'd to find
  Our cable still remain.

As near this place where we did lie,
  Our anchors we 'had dropp'd,
So now we went all hands to work,
  To get the anchor up.

The storm was over, past and gone,
  And being much reviv'd;
Then we for Gibraltar sail'd,
  And soon we there arriv'd.

On board the Hebe frigate then,
  I instantly was sent,
And for Minorca we did sail,
  To join the regiment.

For I the regiment had not seen,
  Since I was sent on shore,
On th' Isle of Howet, when I thought
  I should see them no more.

But now l entertain'd a hope,
  I should see them again;
After all the great fatigues that I
  Had undergone in Spain.

So after sailing for some time,
 The Island we espy'd,
Then we all things to go on shore,
 Did instantly provide.

And as we sailed by the fort,
 All things did strange appear,
And soon our men came flocking down,
 To bid us welcome there.

And soon our ships to anchor came,
 Then we were sent on shore,
So from the dangers of the seas,
 Here I was free once more.

But ah! no gratitude I felt
 Towards the God of grace,
Whose matchless goodness follow'd me,
 And brought me to this place.

I went in barracks here that night,
 And lay till the next day,
Then to my officer I went,
 To ask him for some pay.

At my request he gave me some,
 And liberty he gave,
But oh! I acted like a man
 Who had no soul to save.

My ways and actions they declar'd,
 I did not understand,
That God my actions could discern,
 Upon the sea, and land.

F

That nothing from him could be hid,
  Tho' I did oft rebel,
That he at once might cut me off,
  And send me down to hell.

This island was as bad a place
  As ever I was in,
For drunkenness and swearing too,
  And almost ev'ry sin.

I drank of wine most greedily,
  And rapidly did go
Headlong that road which leads a man,
  To misery and woe.

I liv'd a very wretched life,
  Sin was my element;
When I from liquor was debarr'd,
  Then I was discontent.

Th' inhabitants which here did dwell,
  Appeared very dark,
So that I think it not amiss,
  Some things now to remark.

Now sev'ral months we tarried here,
  And often went to see
Their mode of worship which they had,
  For curiosity.

They do not like the Protestants,
  But call'd us heretics,
Because we would not bow like them,
  Unto the crucifix !

They thought no other way was right,
  For they did all condemn,
Who did not follow their advice,
  And acquiesce with them.

Their love to money it was great,
  And this appear'd quite strange,
For if we went to deal with them,
  'Twas hard to get our change.

And while we tarried in this place,
  I many things did see,
And here the first that struck my mind,
  Was on one good-friday.

The inhabitants of George's town,
  This day appeared grand,
They walked to and fro the streets
  With candles in their hand.

Here was a man which walk'd before,
  A cross upon his back,
And next there followed after him,
  Some women dress'd in black.

Next the apostles they were brought,
  With lamps which burn'd most clear,
And next was Peter and the cock,
  Which closed up the rear.

Priests, monks, and friars, here they walk'd
  With ornaments so fine,
Their garments trimm'd with silver lace,
  Most brilliantly did shine.

And as they walk'd they sung aloud
  Which solemn did appear,
Especially, when night came on,
  Their lights shone bright and clear.

Our men did mock and jeer, and scoff,
  I think this was not right,
For something here doth strike my mind,
  Arising from this sight.

Here I beheld the Son of God,
  From Pilate led away,
With bands of soldiers and the Jews,
  Towards mount Calvary.

Methinks I see the great God-man,
  The only Son of God,
Bearing his cross to Calvary,
  To shed his precious blood.

Here I beheld the harden'd Jews,
  With thorns to make a crown,
And place it on his sacred head,
  Which made the blood run down.

Methinks I see him rise the hill,
  To Calvary ascend,
For sinners there to shed his blood :
  Was ever such a friend ?

And by the mourners that attend,
  Those women here I see,
Which follow'd closely by our Lord,
  When led to Calvary.

I hear his loving words to them,
   " Daughters weep not for me,
" Weep for yourselves, and children dear,
   "And for your family."

Next I beheld him on the cross,
   In agonies and pains,
And view the crimson streams that flow'd;
   To wash us from our stains.

I hear his loving voice proclaim,
   " Forgive my foes, he cried,
" Father! they know not what they do,
   " Tho' me they've crucified."

Again I saw these harden'd Jews,
   When he was ' thirst indeed,
Then vinegar suffus'd with gall,
   They gave him on a reed.

Thus here he hung between two thieves,
   The same did him deride,
But sov'reign grace reach'd one of them,
   And then aloud he cry'd—

" Lord when thou in thy kingdom com'st,
   " Remember me for good,
" Though I have much reviled thee,
   " Yet wash me in thy blood !"

The Saviour listen'd to his cry,
   And said to him in love,
"To day thy soul shall be with me
   " In pardise above."

Thus here the Saviour show'd his love,
   And his almighty pow'r,
In saving this distressed thief,
   When at th' eleventh hour.

But yet these Jews were still unmov'd,
   And for his death did crave,
They cried, " he saved others, but
   " Himself he cannot save."

One of the soldiers with a spear
   Thrust deep into his side,
"' Tis finish'd," then the Saviour said,
   And bow'd his head, and died!

Thus here the Saviour paid that debt
   Which we to justice ow'd,
Fulfil'd that law which we had broke,
   And so made peace with God.

The twelve apostles and the lamps
   Which here did shine so bright,
Did strike me as an emblem of
   That glorious gospel light.

This the apostles preach'd and taught
   To sinners all around,
Exhorting them their sins to leave,
   While mercy might be found.

The Saviour, when he left the dead,
   Commission'd them to preach,
And to go forth through all the world,
   The ignorant to teach.

Th' apostles shone like lights themselves,
  In a benighted world;
Though they were oft abus'd abroad,
  Or into prisons hurl'd.

Though they by men were treated ill
  As Christ their master was;
Yet they rejoiced they were call'd
  To suffer for his cause.

And next, by Peter and the cock,
  Self-confidence I see;
O may this sin be ever kept
  At distance, Lord, from me!

When Jesus spake these words to him,
  "Before the cock crow twice,
"Peter, thou art the very man
  "That will deny me thrice."

But Peter quickly said to him,
  It is not so with me,
"For tho' all men should thee deny,
  "Yet I will follow thee!"

But Peter soon forgot his vow,
  His Master he denied;
But when he heard the cock crow twice,
  He then went out and cried.

But who can tell the state of mind
  That Peter now was in,
When he consider'd how he fell
  Into this awful sin.

But Oh! when Jesus rose again,
    Tho' Peter vilely fell,
He sent to his Disciples, then,
    That they might Peter tell.

What inward joy must Peter feel,
    To hear that Jesus Christ
Had thus remember'd him in love,
    Tho' he denied him thrice.

Methinks I see him stand amaz'd,
    And bow himself in dust,
And cry " O Lord, if I am lost,
    " Thy Judgments would be just!"

" But I repent that I have sinn'd,
    " That I so basely fell,
" And praise that matchless pow'r and love,
    " Which kept me out of hell!"

Thus having made a few remarks,
    I on my way pursue,
That you may see the gracious hand,
    Which safely brought me through.

An expedition now had sail'd,
    As you shall understand,
In order to expel the French
    Out of the Turkish land,

They could us not to Egypt take,
    Because our oath we gave,
To serve five years, or for the war,
    But should not Europe leave.

Often of Egypt have I read,
　But never thought to be
Engaged as a soldier there,
　Or e'er that land to see.

But now there was no room to doubt,
　For it was so design'd,
Our Colonel call'd us to parade,
　Not one to stay behind.

When he addressed us, and said,
　" I hope you'll all agree;
And volunteer your service now
　" To go along with me.

" To help your brother soldiers, who
　" To Egypt now are gone,
"When if it should conclude the war,
　" You'll be discharg'd each one.

" Besides my life is dear to me,
　" As yours is unto you;
" But Oh! my men I cannot doubt
　" But you will all prove true.

" To go to Egypt long with me,
　" Your colours to defend,
" And I will be to each of you
　" A father and a friend.

With one consent we volunteer'd,
　And each one gave his voice
To go to Egypt with him then,
　Which caus'd him to rejoice.

" He said you now shall money have,
  " Some comfort to afford,
" And two days' liberty beside,
  " Before you go on board.

" Then my brave men, I hope you'll **march**
  " Like soldiers for the field,
" Resolv'd once more to meet the foe,
  " And rather die than yield."

But seldom did I think of death,
  Of judgment, or of God,
Or of his goodness, which so oft
  Preserved me abroad.

Instead of calling on the Lord
  To be my strength and shield,
To cover my defenceless head
  When fighting in the field;

I call'd for vengeance to be pour'd
  Upon my guilty head;
And 'twas a mercy that I was
  Not number'd with the dead.

When I my money had receiv'd,
  My heart I must confess,
Nothing could cheer or satisfy,
  But drinking to excess.

Thus here I spent my precious time,
  And all I could afford,
Until the morning was arriv'd
  For me to go on board.

Then we appeared on parade,
　To march down to the quay,
Where all the barges were prepar'd
　To carry us away.

The thirty-first in baracks here
　Appear'd on the parade :
And as we marched on their front,
　Three cheers by us were made.

Then they saluted us again,
　And bid us all good speed;
So we continued marching on,
　On board then to proceed.

We straightway in the Barges went,
　And row'd off along side,
But here we left two men on shore,
　A sea stock to provide.

But when we all got safe on board,
　For sea we did prepare,
And weigh'd our anchors instantly,
　For now the wind was fair.

END OF THE THIRD PART.

PART IV.

An account of the expedition to Egypt—description of several engagements with the French—death of General Abercrombie—the misfortune by which the Author lost his Sight—his departure from Egypt—his danger in a storm which arose during their passage to Malta—his discharge from the Army, and return to England.

WE hoisted sail, past by fort George,
   And bore away to sea,
A frigate call'd the Laminerve,
   Our convoy then to be,

The Kanguroo, a large gun brig,
   Now sail'd in company,
There to defend us, if we should
   Meet with our enemy.

The wind was fair, the weather fine,
   Which did us joy afford,
But as we steer'd our course along,
   A boy fell overboard!

This little boy, the Captain's son,
   Both nimble and expert,
Ran up aloft in time of need,
   Himself then to exert,

But 'ere that he had reach'd the top,
   Ah ! mournful thus to see,
He lost his hold, fell overboard,
   Into the raging sea !

Our Major's cot was on the deck,
   He threw it over board,
In hopes the boy would catch the same,
   Which might relief afford.

But the poor lad was left a-stern,
   The boat was hoisted out,
Whether the boat could live the sea,
   Now each one had a doubt.

The Captain wrung his hands and cried,
   " Alas ! alas ! my son !
" My life I'll venture now for thee,
   " I will all hazards run."

The seamen saw his great distress,
   Resolv'd they were to try,
If they could save his son from death,
   Tho' danger was so nigh.

They row'd towards him with all speed,
   But they were greatly tost,
Which made us sometimes think on board,
   That they would all be lost.

G

God's providence protected them,
  And brought him safe on board,
Which caus'd his father to rejoice,
  To see his son restor'd.

What is impossible with man,
  Is possible with God,
And they his wonders often see,
  Who have been much abroad.

But yet my ignorance was so great,
  When he was brought on board,
That I gave all the praise to man,
  Not thinking of the Lord.

The wind it blew a pleasant gale,
  We Sicily soon spy'd,
And we at Malta did lie to,
  Some things there to provide.

Here soon the boats came off to us,
  To satisfy our need,
And then we soon set sail again,
  For Egypt with all speed.

We had no accident beside
  Befel us, all the way;
For soon the Turkish land we spied
  And anchor'd in the Bay.

The soldiers made their landing good,
  Before we reach'd this place,
But then as we were Volunteers,
  This was no real disgrace.

The land to us appeared strange,
    But there was no delay,
For we were order'd to prepare,
    To go on shore that day.

Our boats we quickly hoisted out,
    We row'd towards the land,
The Turks with many camels stood
    Here waiting on the sand.

Then to assist our baggage on,
    Towards the English camp,
Who did with speed the camels load;
    Then forward we did tramp.

Then soon our countrymen we join'd,
    And pitch'd our tents with speed,
Ready whenever they should march,
    With them there to proceed.

We were immediately inform'd,
    As you shall understand,
The opposition which they had
    Before they reach'd the land.

The Egyptian army in this place,
    The French did oft defy,
And then to drive them back again,
    They many times did try

But they were always forc'd to run,
    And backwards to retreat,
Which made the French much to rejoice,
    The Turks thus to defeat.

G 2

The French the victory oft obtain'd
  Which caus'd the Turks to fear;
And they appeared very glad
  To see our troops land there.

On Sunday Morning, March the eighth,
  The boats along side lay,
In order there to land the troops,
  Before the break of day.

But 'ere that they had reach'd the shore,
  The sun arose so high,
The French perceived them approach,
  Before the boats drew nigh.

Their cannons ready loaded were,
  And formed upon the beach,
So they commenc'd a heavy fire,
  Before the boats could reach.

Their shots, their shells, and musket balls,
  In all directions flew,
But yet our English troops resolv'd,
  That they would venture through.

They killed numbers of our men,
  And wounded numbers more,
And many soldiers here were drown'd,
  Before they reach'd the shore.

But when they got upon the land,
  They soon form'd up in line,
And then to charge upon the French,
  Was quickly their design.

Then with three cheers we made a charge,
  The French soon ran away;
And thus our landing was made good,
  Before the close of day.

The twelfth and thirteenth days again,
  The armies met and fought,
The thirteenth day the French drew back,
  Our troops the vict'ry got.

Then to their batteries they retreat,
  That they awhile might rest;
So then till we were more prepar'd,
  We did not them molest.

General Menew at Cairo was,
  To him they had recourse,
Who made his boast that he would join,
  Their troops to reinforce.

He ordered all his soldiers, that
  They should no pris'ners take,
But they should kill all that they met,
  Or drown them in the lake.

Thus eager for the victory,
  He pressed on that night,
With all his troops in readiness,
  Then to commence the fight.

Thus with all speed he marched on,
  Expecting now to find
The English sleeping in their tents,
  But they were much behind.

By four o'clock that morn did he,
　With all his troops draw nigh;
By ten o'clock they routed were,
　And backwards forc'd to fly.

Our English troops so charged them,
　And put them to the route,
They ran into their batteries,
　And durst not venture out.

But tho' the victory was won,
　And all things seemed well,
Yet soon the mournful news arriv'd,
　That ABERCROMBIE fell!

A musket ball had pierced him,
　And wounded him full sore,
The Faculty at once perceiv'd!
　That he would be no more!

He was a General much esteem'd,
　His soldiers did him love;
It was the wish of every man,
　That he might rest above.

His judgment great, his courage bold,
　While fighting in the field,
But death the conqueror seized him,
　And he was forc'd to yield!

Here death did no distinction make,
　And no respect was paid;
The General with the private man,
　Was on a level laid!

No state of honour can be free,
   From his unerring dart,
He comes at once, and strikes the blow,
   And pierces to the heart !

The high and low, the rich and poor,
   Before this conqueror fall ;
Nor do we know how soon that he
   For each of us may call !

The enemy thus having fled,
   And being now hemm'd in,
Part of our army, then their march,
   For Cairo did begin.

The batt'ries which they had to face,
   I mention them by name ;
St. Juno, and fort Romaney,
   The French possess'd the same.

The battle of fort Ramaney,
   Employ'd them all the day ;
But here the Turks like cowards base,
   Took heels and ran away.

An awful sight presents itself—
   The standing corn took fire,
It burnt with such rapidity,
   Each army did retire !

The enemy soon left their forts,
   That night they all came out;
And for Grand Cairo instantly,
   With speed they took their route.

Our army then pursued them,
  Without the least delay,
And near Grand Cairo pitch'd their tents,
  On he ensuing day.

They saw our men prepare to fight,
  Which caused them to fear;
They did not long resist our force,
  As quickly will appear.

This city they srurender'd up,
  Their spirits being damp'd :—
To Alexandria I return,
  Where I was then encamp'd.

This being now the only place
  The enemy possess'd,
Till we had repossessed the same,
  We could not think of rest.

To shew our situation here,
  Shall be my next design :
Our tents we pitch'd upon the sand,
  Ten regiments in line.

A Mess-house for our Officers,
  We built up with some trees;
And 'midst the branches of the same,
  Blew in the gentle breeze.

Our lines extended near the sea,
  As we lay on the right;
The sun shone very hot by day,
  The dews fell much by night.

The meat was salt which we receiv'd,
  But this was not the worst,
For we had got no water near,
  To satisfy our thirst.

There were no wells within some miles,
  And these could not supply,
Before our vessels were half fill'd,
  The wells were nearly dry.

Some of my readers never knew
  The want of food or drink,
If I should ask them which is worst,
  They would begin to think.

But I who have experienc'd both,
  Will tell them which is worst;
Hunger is sharp, but cannot be
  Compar'd to that of thirst.

But one thing in our favour was,
  They held a market here;
The Turks were forc'd to bring their goods,
  And sell them public there.

Sometimes a mellon we could buy,
  A fruit well fill'd with juice;
This quench'd our thirst when we were dry,
  And was of singular use.

And many diff'rent things were sold,
  By them from day to day;
But I must lay this subject by,
  For duty calls away.

The word was giv'n, now strike your tents,
   And all things here provide,
For we this night must cross the lake,
   And land the other side.

The word was instantly obeyed,
   Without the least delay;
We pack'd up all our baggage then,
   Ready to march away.

Our camels being loaded well,
   We marched to the beach;
But night came on, and it grew dark
   Before we there could reach.

This was what we desired most,
   We did not want the light :
In order to pass unperceiv'd,
   We rather choose the night.

We had to pass so very near
   Our enemies, that we
Resolv'd to keep ourselves that night,
   As still as we could be.

The wind was calm, the waters still
   The stars now gave their light,
And ev'ry thing around us then
   Bespoke a pleasant night.

On board the barges we embark'd
   With speed, but yet with care;
This being done, we left the shore,
   Our little course to steer.

I could not for a moment think
    Of getting any sleep,
As danger was so very near,
    We on our guard must keep.

Our ears were all attention now,
    We look'd towards the shore,
Expecting every hour, that we
    Should hear the cannons roar.

Kind providence protected us,
    And such was now our lot,
That unmolested we arriv'd
    Safe at the destin'd spot.

Thus all was well in this respect;
    But you must understand,
The water was so shallow here,
    We could not reach the land.

But must we in the barges sit
    Until the break of day?
No: we must in the water get,
    Without the least delay.

This being done, our pouches, guns,
    And ammunition store,
To keep them free from damage here,
    We on our shoulders bore.

But having safely reach'd the shore,
    All things were very still;
With cautious steps we moved on
    Towards a large sand hill.

The piquets being order'd out,
 The sentinels were placed;
And then our blankets we prepared,
 To lay us down to rest.

Arm'd and accoutred we lay down,
 Prepar'd for war's alarms;
Expecting soon to hear the word,
 "Arise! stand to your arms."

It was not long before this word
 Saluted all our ears,
"Soldiers, arise, be on your guard,
 "The day-light now appears."

Then we rose immediately,
 And arm'd ourselves like men,
In readiness to meet our foes,
 Should they attack us then.

We found that they made no attempt,
 We look'd towards their line,
And finding they did not advance,
 It now was our design,

To form a camp, and so prepare,
 Without the least delay,
To meet our foes, should they attempt
 To come by night or day.

Each regiment now took up their ground,
 We pitch'd our tents with speed,
And now, to some particulars,
 At once I shall proceed.

The enemy had several forts
   Not far from where we lay,
And we to throw up batteries,
   Did work both night and day.

One day when digging in the sand,
   We met with a surprise;
We found an earthen vessel there,
   Uncommon for its size.

To brake the same was now the cry,
   Each forwarded the plan;
When broke alas! what did we find?
   The bones, of a dead man!

Its size was very large indeed,
   And more then common length,
Which gave us reason to couclnde,
   He was a man of strength.

But was not such a sight as this
   Enough to strike the mind?
This picture of mortality
   A glass for all mankind

Especially for one like me,
   While danger was so near;
Sure I might look into this glass
   And read my features there.

Encompassed with threat'ning death
   Around on every hand,
Not knowing but my bones like his,
   Might soon lie in the sand.

And to confirm the truth of this,
    While we were thus engag'd,
Our enemies percieved us,
    Which made them much enrag'd.

Our muskets being pil'd, we hung
    Our coats upon them then,
Our caps likewise, which we suppos'd
    The French took to be men.

However they commenc'd a fire,
    Their balls around us flew,
But we stood fast, and with all speed,
    We did our works pursue.

We went and took our coats and caps,
    And laid them on the ground,
But while engaged in the same,
    The balls flew swift around.

But one thing here must be remark'd,
    Although they fired then,
In building of this battery,
    We lost none of our men.

They having fired for awhile,
    Without the least success,
They ceas'd the same; when we prepar'd,
    To get in readiness.

I left the battery here that night,
    And only have to say,
The same was quickly made the means
    Of making them give way.

By these few hints you may perceive,
  What soldiers undergo:
But have 1 done with war's alarms?
  Alas! 1 answer, No.

One morning about two o'clock,
  The word was giv'n, "Turn out,"
The same was instantly obey'd,
  When we receiv'd the route.

Thus having got our flints secur'd,
  We marched on our way,
For to attack the battery,
  Before the break of day.

The piquets having joined us,
  The day began to dawn;
Our enemies commenc'd a fire,
  But we kept marching on.

Our orders were to make the charge,
  With this we did comply,
And while engaged in the same,
  The balls did swiftly fly.

We having follow'd up the same,
  The enemy gave way!
I shall hasten to remark,
  What happen'd on that day.

Of what were kill'd and wounded here,
  Is not for me to tell;
Through mercy, 1 escap'd with life,
  And this for me was well.

When all the pris'ners were sent back,
   Our water parties then
Were sent, if possible, to get
   Some water for our men.

When they returned back again,
   We had a small supply,
Which was acceptable to us,
   The heat made us so dry.

It being in the heat of day,
   They much fatigued were,
Which prov'd the death of one of them,
   As quickly you shall hear.

He being almost bath'd in sweat,
   When he was at the well,
He drank of water to excess,
   And awful now to tell—

He was a strong, and able man,
   As any we had got,
But in an instant he fell down,
   And died upon the spot!

How striking to behold a man
   In health before you stand,
But in one hour he now is dead,
   And buried in the sand.

When I reflect on this poor man,
   I can look back and see,
The goodness of a gracious God,
   And say, ah! why not me?

I often wish that soldiers were
   But men of piety;
That they might see the works of God,
   Upon the land and sea.

Should any soldiers read these lines,
   I hope they will attend,
And take advice from one who is
   To them a real friend.

Pray that the Lord would be your strength
   Your succour and your shield,
Pray that he may be your defence,
   When fighting in the field.

Three sins are prevalent with you,
   One is to curse and swear:
O pray that God would give you grace,
   To turn your oaths to pray'r.

Uncleanness is the second sin,
   And drunkenness the third;
Pray that you may forsake them all,
   And turn to Christ the Lord.

You may be valiant for your King,
   And yet be men of pray'r;
And then if call'd to meet the foe,
   You would not have that fear—

Which does possess the minds of all,
   Who enter in the field,
Who never pray that God would be
   Their succour and their shield.

I know at first through fear of death,
　　You eagerly will say,
O Lord have mercy on my soul,
　　And rescue me this day.

But when you have engag'd awhile,
　　You loose all shame and fear,
Your thoughts of death, and judgment too,
　　They quickly disappear.

My brother soldiers, pray reflect
　　Upon your awful state,
Pray to the Lord for pard'ning grace,
　　Before it be too late.

If you are his you need not fear;
　　Tho' death may cut you down,
Your souls to Heav'n shall rise, and three
　　Receive a glorious crown.

Lord, send us more centurions,
　　Upon the land and sea;
Let all our soldiers, seamen too,
　　Be men of piety.

I leave these few imperfect hints,
　　And hasten now to tell,
Whilst I in Egypt did remain,
　　What there to me befel.

'Tis true the great fatigues of war,
　　Were almost at an end;
Because the French to fight with us,
　　Did not again pretend.

The latter end of August month,
  They gave the city up,
This yielded joy, which caused me
  To entertain a hope—

That I should reach the British shore,
  Where I might happy be;
That I might see my friends, and there
  Enjoy their company.

Our able men were all employ'd,
  Relieving every day,
The French from Alexandria,
  That they might go to sea.

Vhe second day it was my lot,
  Which burden was not hard,
To take the dinners to our men,
  Who were that day on guard.

'Tis true the sun shone very hot,
  The sand reflected white;
But I had not a single thought,
  That I should lose my sight.

As I drew near the city gates,
  While viewing of the walls,
A blast of wind blew in my eyes,
  Which seem'd like burning coals.

Immediately I felt a pain,
  In one, or both my eyes;
This very much discouraged me,
  And fill'd me with surprise.

That I should lose my eye-sight now,
  Was much upon my mind,
As many of my countrymen
  Had lately been struck blind.

The water gushed from my eyes,
  The inflamation strong,
The snn shone bright, so that I scarce
  Could find my way along.

When I arrived at the place,
  The soldiers saw my state,
And wish'd that I might get relief,
  Before it was too late.

But when I came again to camp,
  My pain was very great,
One eye was swelled very much,
  And in a constant heat.

I waited on a surgeon then,
  The nearest to that place;
But who I since had cause to think,
  Was ign'rant of my case.

From him I could get no relief,
  Thus in this wretched plight
I then returned to my tent,
  And spent a mournful night.

How glad was I when morning came,
  Hoping to get some ease,
But by that time the other eye
  Had taken the disease.

The serjeant soon came by, and call'd
 The blind from every tent,
Then we took hold each other's coats,
 And to the doctor's went.

The doctor having view'd my case,
 Order'd me instantly
To go into the hospital,
 With which I did comply.

Five blisters I must have applied
 About my head and eyes;
But what did more augment my pain,
 The place so swarm'd with flies.

In order to afford relief,
 Experiments were tried,
Large poultices and likewise drops
 Were frequently applied.

But these prov'd ineffectual,
 My eye-sight to restore,
And sometimes I had painful thoughts
 That I should see no more.

Thus sev'ral days and weeks I spent,
 Rack'd with distressing pain,
And scarcely thought it possible,
 I should my sense retain.

Oft have I wish'd that some one would,
 With pistol, sword, or knife;
In order to relieve my pain,
 Cut short my wretched life.

But blessed be the God of love,
  Who did not at this time,
In answer to my rash request,
  Cut me off in my prime.

Now all things being reconcil'd,
  November month was come,
Which made our troops begin to think
  About returning home.

The doctors entertain'd a hope,
  That when we left this place,
Another climate might produce
  Much diff'rence in our case.

This very much encourag'd us,
  We thought it might be so;
I waited but impatiently
  The time when we should go.

Soon after this, the orders came,
  To take us who were dark
With care down to the water side,
  In order to embark.

This gratified us very much,
  The officers were kind;
They now stood by in readiness,
  To help the helpless blind.

The officers of diff'rent rank
  Did now themselves exert,
They guided us into the boats,
  Lest any should be hurt.

On board the Vestal frigate I
　　Was carefully convey'd;
The soldiers being all embark'd,
　　Our anchors soon were weigh'd.

Thus having all things now prepar'd,
　　For Malta we set sail;
And what prov'd fortunate for us,
　　It blew a pleasant gale.

As soon as we put off to sea,
　　My eyes began to swell;
And I in reason could not think
　　They ever would be well.

They now were frightful to behold,
　　Worse than they were at first;
And this opinion now prevail'd,
　　They certainly must burst.

A fellow sufferer and me
　　Were put in the sick bay,
There in a dreadful agony,
　　We pass'd our time away.

The major he was now on board,
　　Whose kindness I revere;
He often came to visit us,
　　As with a parent's care.

Nothing particular occurr'd
　　During this voyage at sea,
Only we lost an aged man—
　　Death summon'd him away.

We had some heavy squalls of wind,
　But chiefly proving fair,
Kind providence protecting us,
　We on our course did steer.

At length the pleasing news was heard,
　That Malta was in sight,
Which gave us reason to believe.
　We should be there that night.

The twelfth day of December was
　The time when we arriv'd,
To take us all on shore that night,
　They instantly contriv'd.

Our ship, she being safely moor'd,
　The boats were now employ'd;
We then were guided in the same,
　And to the shore convey'd

I went in barracks for the night
　Then to the hospital,
My eyes were now much easier,
　Tho' far from being well.

The swelling being almost gone,
　The inflammation ceas'd,
And though I still remain'd as blind,
　I was from pain releas'd.

Our regiment then disembark'd,
　They went in barracks here,
And soon the orders came to them
　That they might volunteer.

Our officers had still a hope
　　That we should see again;
And offer'd us a bounty, if
　　We would with them remain.

Some of our blind men now refus'd,
　　What I esteem'd a prize,
Altho' I knew my servitude,
　　Depended on my eyes.

I scarcely gave these things a thought,
　　But felt myself inclin'd,
And went and took a bounty then,
　　With sev'ral of the blind.

Then to the wine house I repair'd,
　　My mind was fully bent,
That I would have an ample store,
　　Of wine and akedent.*

Thus wretchedly I spent my time
　　In drinking, swearing too;
Without reflecting on the hand
　　Which thus far brought me through.

My bounty being nearly spent,
　　The month of March was come,
When we receiv'd the welcome news,
　　That we were going home.

Before the general Officers,
　　We were examin'd then,
Who when they had inspected us,
　　Discharg'd us as blind men.

* A liquor.

I

Our Sergeants, they were order'd now
   To settle all our pay,
And we had orders to embark
   For England the next day.

Next morning, being all prepar'd,
   Our comrades did attend,
That they might bid us all farewell,
   And their assistance lend

Sergeants, and Corp'rals, privates too,
   Walk'd with us to the place,
Whose kindness manifested then,
   Time never can efface.

Our Officers likewise stood by,
   And lent a helping hand,
Wish'd us our sight, and safe return
   To England's happy land.

They helped us into the boats,
   Protection we implor'd,
We then lanch'd off, bade them farewell,
   And soon got safe on board.

Our Colonel came on board and ask'd,
   If we were satisfied,
" Have you receiv'd your just demands,"
   " Yes, Sir," we all replied.

Our anchors being nearly up,
   He bade us all farewell :—
What happen'd on our passage home,
   I hasten now to tell.

The sixth of March we hoisted sail,
  Which month we oft remark,
Produces heavy gales of wiud,
  With stormy nights, and dark.

We had not sailed but three days,
  If I remember right,
When we were overtaken with
  A dreadful storm by night.

Of being damag'd by the same,
  Our captain did not fear,
But what he dreaded most was this,
  A large king's ship was near.

He knew if she run foul of us,
  No human aid could save,
She certainly would run us down—
  The sea must be our grave.

As we were blind, we lay below,
  With all attentive ears,
At length we heard the captain cry,
  Which much increas'd our fears.

" Lash, lash the helm, and each prepare,
  For your approaching end,
For we are lost, lost, lost, he cried,
  And none can us befriend !"

The women shriek'd, while some replied
  Ah none ! ah none can save ,
The ship must sink, and all therein
  Must share a wat'ry grave !

Immediately we heard a crash,
  Which seem'd towards our bow,
Which caused some to think and say,
  Ah! we are sinking now!

What consternation fill'd each breast;
  But, lo! we heard a cry,
Our damage is but very small,
  The ship has pass'd us by.

Our captain, he fresh courage took;
  In this he did confide,
That having now got much sea room,
  We should the storm outride.

Our bow sprit being damag'd, they
  Soon put it in repair,
The storm decreas'd, our hope reviv'd,
  And homeward we did steer.

Nothing particular occur'd
  Through all our voyage beside;
Only there were some of our men,
  With a short illness died.

We had an aged man on board,
  Who with a father's care,
Often came down to visit us,
  And ask us how we were.

We having missed him one day,
  Our men felt a desire,
To know the reason why he did
  Not after us enquire.

Alas! the answer we receiv'd,
  Did no relief afford,
We found that he fell sick and died,
  And was thrown overboard.

How justly then may it be said,
  Respecting feeble man,
His days fly swiftly as the wind,
  His life is but a span.

We call'd at Gibraltar, where
  We made but a short stay,
We sent aboard to fetch some wine,
  And then we sail'd away.

Thus having once more put to sea,
  I did my thoughts employ,
Anticipating when at home,
  What I should there enjoy.

However, in process of time,
  As you shall understand,
We knew by what the seamen said,
  That we drew near to land.

The truth of which was soon affirm'd,
  Which yielded us delight,
To hear the seamen now exclaim,
  That land appear'd in sight.

Some having asked what land it was,
  Being answer'd by a friend,
We understood the land in sight,
  Was that of the land's end.

Such was the language of my heart,
　Adieu all care and toil,
I soon shall meet with all my friends,
　Upon my native soil.

Of being lost upon the sea,
　Who did not fear nor dread,
Then up the channel steer'd our course,
　And made towards Spithead.

When we had reach'd the mother bank,
　And came to anchor there,
Then we to ride to quarantine,
　Did instantly prepare.

As we had several men that died,
　Upon our passage home,
In consequence of which we now,
　Must lie three weeks to come.

'Tis true the boats came off to us,
　From them we were supplied,
As most of us had money then,
　We did good things provide.

The master of the quarantine,
　Came off the twentieth day,
He hail'd the officers on board,
　And thus to them did say—

" Of salt water give each a pint,
　Not one man must you spare,
And we to take you all on shore,
　To morrow shall prepare.

"Your necessaries must be burnt,
　　Should you have more or less,
And such shall be provided with
　　A suit of flannel dress"

At first we thought this saying hard,
　　But it was very right,
In order that all ill effects,
　　Might be avoided quite.

Next day the the weather being fair,
　　The boats along side came,
Then we were wash'd from head to foot
　　And lower'd in the same.

We being cloath'd, the boats push'd off,
　　And what gave us delight,
We soon were landed at West Cowes,
　　Upon the Isle of White.

To Park-House barracks we were led,
　　There we awhile must lie,
The people stood and pitied us
　　As we were passing by.

What cause had I to thank the Lord,
　　For all his mercies past,
In that he had preserved me,
　　And brought me safe at last.

About a fortnight we remain'd
　　In barracks at this place,
But here I acted like a man,
　　Quite destitute of grace.

The doctors then examin'd us,
  And quickly gave the word,
That we to London must be sent,
  Where we should pass the board.

Those who receiv'd a little sight,
  Might walk if so inclin'd,
But a small vessel was prepar'd,
  To carry all the blind.

Then we were sent on board again,
  The wind blew a fair gale,
And having got our anchors up,
  For London we set sail.

When we at Greenwich safe arriv'd,
  We cast our anchors there,
Into the barges we were sent,
  And forward we did steer.

As night was coming on apace,
  Each one bound up their eyes;
We sailed under London bridge,
  And Westminster likewise.

Between the hours of twelve and one,
  We reach'd the destin'd shore,
When I with care was help'd thereon,
  To cross the seas no more.

Some men came down to our relief,
  I thought this looked well,
In order to conduct us safe,
  To Chelsea hospital.

The men conducted us with care,
   And led us to the place;
The kindness I received there,
   Time cannot well erase.

Each being seated on a bed,
   We thought that we were blest,
And when we had refresh'd ourselves,
   We all retir'd to rest.

Thus having gain'd refreshing sleep,
   When call'd and bid to rise,
We scarcely knew where we were got,
   Which fill'd us with surprise,

O how desirable is rest,
   Upon the sea or land;
Those who support a place like this,
   Our warmest thanks demand.

Here I was us'd as well as man
   Could ever wish to be,
Yea, all of us were treated with
   Great hospitality.

We asked when we should go home,
   They answer'd very soon,
And told us they should pass the board,
   The seventh day of June.

This was the Monday following,
   When many of the blind,
Were led from Chelsea to the place,
   By men who acted kind.

The people stood, and pitied us,
  As very well they might,
Yea, some of the nobility,
  Were moved at the sight.

Their kindness to us they made known,
  Our case they did lament;
When money with some handkerchiefs,
  They did to us present.

Thus being treated with respect,
  This did relief afford,
We thank'd them kindly for the same,
  Then went and pass'd the board.

A pension they allowed us,
  Which satisfied us well;
Then we were all conducted back,
  Into the hospital.

The Duke of York, whose kindness then,
  I always shall revere,
He acted like a soldier's friend,
  And with a parent's care!

All our accounts were settled up,
  And every man was paid,
And the expence for riding home,
  Our government defray'd.

In the road waggon I was book'd,
  And one pound six was paid,
In order that I might with care,
  Be to my home convey'd.

About the hour of twelve o'clock,
　For Cornwall I set out,
With six blind passengers beside,
　All taking the same rout.

I was eight nights upon the road,
　Which much fatigued me,
Before I reach'd the long sought place,
　Of my nativity.

But when I enter'd the last stage,
　I thought to be there soon;
And I arrived safe at home,
　The twenty-first of June.

My friends at home were all surpris'd,
　Not knowing of my case;
I sent two letters, but I found
　Not one had reach'd this place.

They had not heard a word from me,
　For more than two long years,
They thought me dead, but my return
　Soon banish'd all their fears.

END OF THE FOURTH PART.

PART V.

The Author's reflections on the providential dispensations of God towards him—his dissolute Life after his return—his conversion to God, and his christian experience, down to the present time—concluding with a prayer for his King and Country.

GREAT God! since I that mercy found,
   Which comes alone from thee,
Help me to tell to sinners round,
   What thou hast done for me.
My christians soldiers' you will see,
   While I attempt to trace,
The goodness of the Lord to me,
   The riches of his grace.
When but a child, his love to me
   Surpassed every thought,
My mother died, yet I by him,
   Was up to manhood brought.

When for a Soldier I engag'd,
  And cross'd the wat'ry deep ;
When threat'ning billows foam'd and rag'd,
  His hand did safely keep.

In Holland, Ireland, and in Spain,
  Likewise in Egypt too,
His gracious hand did me sustain,
  And led me safely through.

He brought me back from Egypt's coast,
  With his almighty pow'r,
And although blind, yet I can trace
  His goodness to this hour.

O what abundant cause have I
  To praise his holy name ;
Alas ! I acted quite reverse
  And own it to my shame.

His long-forbearing love to me,
  Had not the least effect ;
I to his people or his ways,
  Had not the least respect.

Incapable of all employ,
  I now took great delight,
In frequenting the alehouse, where,
  I spent both day and night.

I thought no one could equal me,
  As I had been abroad ;
I chose the company of those
  Who liv'd estrang'd from God.

The company I chose were such
  Who should both sing and swear,
I spent my time with them, as if
  There were no God to fear.

Many were very kind to me,
  Which kindness prov'd my hurt;
They lov'd my company, because
  I did their minds divert.

By singing warlike songs to them,
  Respecting land and sea,
Thus I was deem'd by them as one,
  They call'd good company.

Unto this wicked course of life,
  I was addicted so ;
When through necessity debarr d,
  I knew not what to do.

Those who reprov'd me for my faults,
  I call'd my enemies ;
Their good advice I would not take,
  Their counsels did despise.

I often stray'd for many miles,
  In order that I might
Do what I pleas'd without controul,
  Should it be wrong or right.

When I had tarried many days,
  My friends they sometimes thought,
That I some day should be found dead,
  And to my home be brought.

When I expended what I had,
　　Then I returned home,
And bid defiance unto all
　　Who talk'd, or near me come.

"Twas near four years I acted thus,
　　Not fearing God or man;
Ing'rant of his works and ways,
　　And of Salvation's plan.

Tho' many times when very drunk,
　　While lying on my bed,
A form of Prayer I knew by heart,
　　Repeatedly I said.

When I this duty had perform'd,
　　I thought all things were right;
Yes, more than this, I felt secure,
　　Should I expire that night.

What depths of ign'rance I display'd,
　　To think that feeble plea,
Would fit my sould for sudden death,
　　And for a judgment day.

' Tis true, I did not persecute
　　The people of the Lord;
But felt inclin'd, and sometimes went
　　To hear a preached word.

But what induced them to hear,
　　I scarcely could conceive,
That preachers were of any use,
　　I did not then believe.

But God, the great, the only wise,
    Look'd down and pitied me,
His loving kindness he display'd,
    And gave me eyes to see.

It is about five years ago,
    Returning home one night,
When I had spent all that I had,
    And in a dreadful plight!

I thought while going on the road,
    When I returned home,
How I could answer all of those,
    Who to reprove me come.

But God was now about to stop
    Me in my mad career ;—
But in a very striking way,
    As quickly you shall hear.

All on a sudden, I was seiz'd,
    With trembling and with fear;
Nor could I put those thoughts from me,
    But danger now seem'd near.

I thought the clouds then gather'd black,
    Extending o'er my head,
I thought the lightning now would flash,
    And I should be struck dead!

Darkness and horror grief and shame,
    Oppress'd my guilty mind,
I ran, and wept, I cry'd aloud.
    But no relief could find.

My sins arose before my view,
   I felt the heavy load,
Upwards I durst not lift my eyes,
   Where dwelt an angry God.

If I look'd downward, there was hell
   Presented to my view,
In this distress I cry'd aloud,
   Alas! what shall I do?

All thoughts of ever being sav'd,
   Were far remov'd from me;
To think of ever reaching home,
   I thought this could not be.

But he who rich in mercy is,
   My worthless life did spare,
In mercy he preserved me,
   And brought me safely there.

But when my friends reproved me
   I durst not say a word;
They being ign'rant of my case,
   Could no relief afford.

They saw my grief, and seem'd surpris'd
   That I was now so still,
Because I did not answer them,
   They thought I had been ill.

My father was a moral man,
   But destitute of grace,
I then saw no utility,
   In telling him my case.

I labour'd under doubts and fears,
  But felt myself inclin'd,
To go and hear, if possible,
  I might some comfort find.

All kind reproof I now could bear,
  Made willing to be teach'd;
And often with God's people went,
  To hear the gospel preach'd.

'Tis true I felt the word condemn,
  I saw and and felt my state,
But sometimes entertain'd a hope,
  That I was not too late.

Some, who had known my conduct past,
  On me look'd very shy,
" Is Saul among the prophets now ?"
  Some people loud would cry !

But when they saw the change divine,
  The bless'd effects of grace,
They pointed me to Jesus Christ,
  And bid me seek his face.

I sought the Lord by fervent pray'r,
  That he would bless my soul,
That he would give my conscience peace,
  And make the sinner whole.

One day when on my bended knees,
  Engag'd in earnest pray'r,
The Lord shone in upon my mind,
  And banish'd all my fear.

He said, I will be merciful,
  I will thy sins forgive,
My Son hath ransom'd thee from death,
  He died that thou might'st live.

A glorious train of promises,
  Did now my mind o'erflow,
I wished then that all the world,
  Did this salvation know.

Thus I enjoy'd this peace of mind,
  For sev'ral weeks at least,
I thought my troubles all were past,
  And every conflict ceas'd.

But by and by, the tempter came,
  I felt an evil heart,
The things I thought were all destroy'd,
  Were but subdued in part.

This cause'd me to be much in pray'r,
  To ask for strength'ning grace,
I pray'd that God would guide my feet
  Through all my christian race.

I felt his promises applied,
  Well suited to my case,
I always found his pow'r could save,
  When I could trust his grace,

But I have reason to lament,
  When I his goodness see,
In that I have not serv'd him more,
  Who did so much for me.

I know, had I more faithful been
  To that which he has giv'n,
I should enjoy more peace within,
  That sweet foretaste of heav'n.

But glory be ascrib'd to him,
  That yet he doth me spare:
And still I find a pressing need,
  For watchfulness and pray'r,

I love his people, and his house,
  His word, his works, and ways;
And in his service hope to spend,
  The remnant of my days.

When first I knew the love of God,
  My friends I did reprove:
But they would not receive my word,
  Tho' it was done in love.

They did not love my company,
  Reproof they could not bear,
But order'd me to quit the house,
  And go to lodge elsewhere.

Now these and many other things,
  Did much affect my mind,
Which did appear more hard to me,
  Because I now was blind.

This being tried, I often thought
  It was the case with me,
That I with strangers always meet
  With most civility.

I tarried not long after this,
   When I remov'd from there,
I came by water, and by stage,
   As far as Dorsetshire.

At Bridport I took lodgings then,
   And met with people there,
Who I have reason to believe,
   Worshipp'd the Lord with fear.

One day, when walking in the street,
   Some person spoke to me,
Which prov'd to be a gentleman,
   Nam'd Samuel Grundry.

When he had ask'd how I came blind,
   He told me, in that town
There was a man well skill'd in eyes,
   Whose name was Doctor Down.

He gave me his respects to him,
   And bade me then apply,
And ask him if he thought he could
   Restore to me one eye.

Tell him, quoth he, if this be done,
   I will the charge defray;
I thank'd him for his friendly aid,
   And went to him straightway.

The Doctor view'd my eyes, and said,
   That they were too far gone,
He said had I apply'd at first,
   He might have saved one.

I thanked Mr. Grundry in
  A poem on his name;
To me he ten and sixpence gave,
  A present for the same.

Some foreign soldiers lying here,
  The German Doctor thought,
When one day looking at my eyes,
  A cure might yet be wrought.

He tried to couch one of my eyes,
  Which caused me much pain,
But this with several other means,
  Alas, prov'd all in vain!

Six months in Bridport, I remain'd,
  And got acquainted there,
With one who was a native of
  Pitsford, Northamptonshire.

I found he meant to leave this place,
  And then 'twas soon agreed,
That there together we should go,
  If God our way should speed.

I liv'd with him about three months,
  When we remov'd from there,
And came to London, and from thence,
  Into Northamptonshire.

At Boughton then we went to live,
  And being settled there,
I lived with him in this place,
  For nearly half a year.

I changed my condition then,
  And took to me a wife,
For whom I now feel gratitude,
  And for a settled life.

O may the Lord direct our feet,
  Through this dark wilderness,
Grant us in every time of need,
  His all-sufficient grace.

Help us to live and walk in love,
  I humbly, Lord, implore;
Prepare our souls to meet above,
  When time shall be no more!

Since then to London I have been,
  In order that I might
Procure, if possible, some means,
  To gain a little sight.

But finding every effort fail,
  I beg to be resign'd,
Knowing it is the will of God,
  That I should still be blind.

Readers, before I close these lines,
  I would you all remind,
I was but twenty one years old,
  When first I came home blind.

The years I serv'd his Majesty,
  Were very nearly three;
And every line composed here,
  I made from memory.

Lord! grant thy blessing on the same,
 Let every reader be,
Led to admire that matchless grace,
 Which found out worthless me.

Like chosen Israel of old,
 When out of Egypt freedt
Jehovah through the wilderness,
 Supply'd their every need.

I thought my residence was fix'd,
 To strike my tent no more,
Till I should leave this wilderness,
 To land on Canaan's shore.

I liv'd at Boughton near three years,
 When I remov'd from thence;
But I in every step can trace,
 The hand of providence.

Having a place provided by
 A friend in Bedfordshire,
Who liv'd at Ampthill at that time,
 We came and settled there.

I found a people in that town,
 Whose kindness shewn to me,
Nor time nor distance ever can
 Efface from memory.

I was much gratified to find,
 The gospel preached there,
And numbers in that place inclin'd,
 To go the same to hear.

I also found a pious few,
　With whom I shortly join'd,
And oft while worshipping with them,
　True happiness did find.

My soul was quicken'd in this place,
　To run the heavenly road,
And I more fully did resolve,
　To give myself to God.

Nine months I tarried in this place,
　And oft rejoiced to see,
The Lord reviving his own work,
　In our society.

Here I had no abiding place,
　Nor must I here remain,
But I must once more strike my tent,
　Arise and march again.

I with reluctance left this town,
　For Bedford, where I live,
For when I think upon these friends,
　My warmest thanks I give.

To Boughton and to Ampthill,
　Bedford and friends around,
Who bought a mangling machine,
　Which I of service found.

Lord, what am I that thou shouldst give
　Such friends in every place,
For me the chief of sinners—me,
　Not worthy of thy grace.

My daily bread to me is given,
　My water it is sure,
Help me to put my trust in thee,
　Nor doubt thy goodness more.

O may it be my chief employ
　To praise my father God,
O may I never want a tongue,
　To sound his praise abroad.

I shall conclude this narrative,
　With love and charity,
By offering a feeble pray'r,
　For my King and country.

God bless the King, support his mind,
　Remove disease and pain,
Return him to his wonted health,
　And grant him long to reign.

God bless the Queen, the Regent Prince,
　And all that family,
With wisdom which comes from above,
　And inward piety.

When call'd to lay their honours down,
　Grant them to meet above ;
May each receive a glorious crown,
　And praise redeeming love.

Bless all the great men of our land,
　In their behalf appear,
Help them to govern this our Isle,
　In thy most holy fear.

Bless all the rich, of every rank,
  May they thy goodness see ;
Help them, as faithful stewards here,
  To act with charity.

Bless all our officers on land,
  And those upon the sea,
May all our soldiers, seamen, too,
  Be men of piety.

Bless all the poor, and fatherless,
  The tempted and distress'd :
Great God ! supply their every want,
  And calm each troubled breast.

Bless all thy preachers from on high,
  Who may dispense thy word,
May they in faithfulness declare
  The counsel of the Lord.

Enlighten all benighted lands,
  The wand'ring Jews call home ;
Be this the pray'r of every heart,
  " Lord, let thy kingdom come."

Hasten the time when all shall know ;
  Thy well beloved Son,
Extend thy truth, maintain thy pow'r,
  And let thy will be done.

THE END.

J. Haddon, Printer, Tabernacle Walk, London.